Mindfulness

Health and Serenity

A Practical Guide on How to Find Yourself in a Crazy World

Introduction

Life in the twenty-first century is full of chaos and fatigue. With the advent of technology and machines, our lives have become easier physically, but what about our mind and soul? The tiresome tasks that took our ancestors days and months to finish are performed by us with automatic machines in the blink of an eye.

Still, we are always short of time. We have become so mechanical that we do not have time for ourselves. Always rushing to complete tasks, trying to be more, and pushing ourselves to follow societal norms has somehow taken a toll on our wellbeing, and we feel misplaced in this crazy world. We feel disconnected, confused, and stressed from within, but we don't really know why.

The root of the problem lies in not knowing who you are and finding serenity in your life. The good news is this issue comes with a solution in the form of mindfulness.

Mindfulness is living in the present moment having the energy of being more aware and awake in every moment of our life. It is about intentionally trying to bring our body and mind into harmony while performing routine activities in our daily life, so you understand who you are and what you want in life.

Mindfulness does not happen overnight. It comes with continuous practice and deliberate efforts. This book will teach you how to be mindful and why this is important. In an era of the internet and gadgets, let us indulge in the beauty of every moment and learn to be more kind, gentle, and compassionate towards life and whatever it brings to us. Welcome to this enduring journey of mindfulness!

This document is geared towards providing exact and reliable information in regards to the topic and issue covered. The publication is sold with the idea that the publisher is not required to render accounting, officially permitted or otherwise qualified services. If advice is necessary, legal or professional, a practiced individual in the profession should be ordered.

- From a Declaration of Principles which was accepted and approved equally by a Committee of the American Bar Association and a Committee of Publishers and Associations.

The information provided herein is stated to be truthful and consistent, in that any liability, in terms of inattention or otherwise, by any usage or abuse of any policies, processes, or directions contained within is the solitary and

Table of Contents

Chapter 1: Finding Yourself In This Crazy World

During a busy workday, shouldn't you stop for a while and reflect on where you are heading? You are always over-occupied and hyperactive, performing multiple tasks simultaneously. Thinking about the past and worrying about the future, you forget to live in the present.

You need to understand that the present is what you have in your hands. You can neither change your mistakes of the past nor have any control over what is going to happen in the future. You can be sure of only your present and what you achieve today.

So why not try to find yourself in this crazy world?

What Does it Mean to Find Yourself?

Finding yourself in this world with all its madness means to slow down, understand who you are, explore your aspirations and make your life more about yourself.

Your mind is complicated and needs a conscious effort on your part to make it efficient and productive. Research shows that when you are awake but not keenly paying attention to any task, the 'Default Mode' of your brain turns on. This involves your brain operating on 'automatic pilot', causing mental babble and mind wandering. Thus, you tend to dwell more on the past and distress about the future, judging and criticizing a lot.

Default mode activates particular areas of your brain, including the brain's "fear center" (the amygdala). This activation mechanism thus results in understanding the world around you through opinions and thoughts instead of your senses. It is being associated closely with mental health issues, including stress, depression, anxiety, ADHD, and even autism and schizophrenia. It also hinders your cognitive ability, weakens academic and occupational functioning. Another difficulty is to understand others and communicate effectively.

In contrast, when you are attentively involved in what you are doing, different parts of your brain are engaged that make you deeply feel the things through your senses. You give up on distressing, anticipating, judging, and fighting reactively. You can practice this way of active living while exercising, listening to music, driving, observing nature, enjoying your hobbies, and spending time with near and dear ones. In such moments, you effortlessly exist in the present and fully engage in the senses.

For most people, life is getting demanding and hectic nowadays. Technology keeps you on your toes, and there isn't much time to just 'be yourself.' You are often doing multiple things at the same time: texting while reading a book, eating while watching tv, or even looking at your phone while taking a long walk. You are working late hours and bringing work home.

All this chaos takes you farther from who you truly are and everything you wish to do in life. To let go of the stress, hurt, pain, and lack of contentment in life, you need to find out your genuine self. It is only then that you will realize your true nature, the things that bring you pure joy, the difference between your real and superficial desires, and the need to slow down to just enjoy the moment.

When you find yourself, you slowly figure out your sense of purpose. You know what you want from your life, the things that spark joy for you, and the people that mean the world to you. Slowly, you start to surround yourself with the right things, people, and activities, and your life starts to brim with joy.

Let us now discuss how mindfulness can help you achieve this in the following chapter.

Chapter 2: Mindfulness And Its Importance In Your Life

Life feels harsh, brutal, and distressing at times. The world sometimes only seems full of suffering, violence, greed, and hunger. Everyone is fighting and striving for survival. All this tends to stress you out.

While we cannot always control everything that happens around us, we can improve how it affects us. Mindfulness is a very effective technique to alleviate this stress and enjoy life to its fullest.

But what exactly is mindfulness? Is it a medicine or a magic potion? Therapy or a remedy? Let us find that out.

Understanding Mindfulness

Evidence shows that mindfulness is none of the aforementioned things. That said, it has the power to make you feel light-hearted and content. It teaches you how to be conscious of and cherish little things in life. Little gestures of love like little drops of rain can make your life wonderful in meaningful ways. It is just a matter of seeking happiness and spreading it in every moment, and mindfulness allows you to do that.

Mindfulness is a "mode of living" that is deep-rooted in focusing deliberately and non-judgmentally on the present moment. It implies that the mind is fully concentrating on what's happening within yourself and in the outer world. It requires you to actively engage in your daily life with a cautious and attentive mind.

You have to guard your thoughts while doing your routine tasks; otherwise, your mind wanders around and distracts you from the task. This is how you lose focus on the moment and start worrying about the past or future.

Mindfulness is a virtue that every human being naturally bears; it's not something you have to invoke; you just have to learn how to implement it.

Founder of Buddhism and renowned mystic, Buddha once said,

"The secret of health for both mind and body is not to mourn for the past, worry about the

future, or anticipate troubles, but to live in the present moment wisely and earnestly."

The Science of Mindfulness

Mindfulness has now evolved as a mental science and is studied as a significant factor in reducing stress and enhancing overall happiness. It starts with focusing on the moment and develops by connecting with other elements that cultivate a conscious, mindful experience.

These elements are described below:

- **Awareness:** Paying deliberate attention to everything that you see, hear, smell or touch and taste. To be aware of the moment, you need to dive into minute details of things that we usually ignore.

- **Focus:** Learning to focus on what is happening in the present moment without giving a thought to the past or future. It is when we focus on the moment at hand that we realize its beauty and importance in our life.

- **Acceptance:** When you become aware and focused, you develop an innate feeling of acceptance and openness to every new experience. Instead of shunning new ideas, you become open to exploring them. Instead of labeling emotions and thoughts as good or bad, you accept them as to how you experience them.

- **Observation:** Observation refers to objectively observing your unpleasant feelings and thoughts without reacting or judging. Conscious observation helps you understand and explore different perspectives related to a situation, idea, object, and even person.

By incorporating these elements of mindfulness in your life, you are able to cultivate a mindful state of mind that brings forth the following improvements in your life.

The Benefits of Mindfulness

Mindfulness offers you a time in your life when you stop judging and explore the mechanism of the mind with curiosity and free will. It transforms the way how you approach life, making you more a warm and kind to yourself and others.

Mindfulness brings with it countless benefits that include:

- Reducing stress

- Boosting performance

- Giving you a deep insight and attentiveness through reading your mind,

- Increasing consciousness of others' wellbeing.

- Balancing emotional wellbeing

- Bringing positive changes in attitudes and behaviors

- Nurturing relationships

- Improving happiness and health

- Increasing resilience

- Reducing anxiety and depression

- Slowing down the aging process

- Reducing a physical pain and fatigue

- Uncovering your own blind spots

- Improving sleep quality

- Cultivating a focused approach

Mindfulness is likely to become a transformative social trend in coming times because anyone can practice it. It is easy to practice mindfulness, as it involves innate human qualities, and anyone can learn without changing their beliefs. It is not just a practice but a way of living. As you confront this world's increasing complication and uncertainty, mindfulness can escort you to valuable and low-cost solutions to definite problems.

Mindfulness as a Practice

Professor emeritus Jon Kabat-Zin founded Stress Reduction Clinic at the University of Massachusetts Medical Center and put into practice 'mindfulness meditation' as 'conventional medicine.' He proved that practicing mindfulness improves both physical and psychological health and brings positive changes in your lifestyle.

Applying the techniques of mindfulness and self-engagement to real-life problems is a challenging task. Yet you can learn it with resilience and perseverance.

Here are some mindfulness-based activities that you can get started with:

1. *Mindful Breathing*

You can start with simpler activities like closing your eyes for a couple of minutes and concentrate on your breathing pattern. 3-Minute Breathing Space is a perfect practice for those with busy lives and occupied minds. The exercise comprises three one-minute sessions and works as follows:

1. The first minute is consumed with answering the question "How am I doing right now?" while concentrating on the feelings, thoughts, and sensations you experience and trying to translate those into words.

2. The second minute involves keeping yourself aware of the breath.

3. The last minute is involved in an extension of attention outward from the breath, feeling how your breathing influences the rest of the body.

Concentrating your attention on a simple thing like your breath can take some regulation and practice. Your mind will probably roam off many times. When it does, simply take note of it and, without passing judgment, bring your awareness back to the present.

2. Mindfulness Eating

Another task is to focus on what you eat. Instead of eating it quickly without thinking much, slow down. Hold it in your hand, smell it, and feel it in your fingers. Place it on your tongue and taste it. After that, eat it slowly, paying attention to how it feels and tastes. Observe thoughts or sensations that you come across as you eat.

3. Mindfulness Walking

Mindful walking is done on purpose. The focus is to help you better manage the internal and external distractions that block our path to mental happiness.

A mindful walk is comprised of three elements —
walking, talking, and mindfulness. Whether you
walk alone or in the company, the mindfulness
element is about concentrating on the things
which we may miss out on in the business of daily
life.

4. Mindfulness-based Observation

Mindful observation starts with selecting a
natural object from your environment and
focusing on it for a minute or two; this could be
anything such as an insect, clouds, the moon, a
tree, flower, and just about anything.

Look carefully at this object as if you are seeing it
for the first time. Now allow yourself to resonate
with its energy and its purpose within the natural
world.

Some other proven techniques that help you
cultivate mindfulness are as follows.

1. Engaging in meditation while sitting,
   standing, or walking

2. Inserting short pauses into everyday life;

3. Merging other activities with meditation, such as yoga or sports

All of these techniques compel you to slow down and keep your focus on the present moment. With that awareness, you can better focus on your thoughts and build a positive mindset. Let us discuss that in the next chapter.

Chapter 3: Build A Positive Mindset

Mindfulness is closely linked to positive psychology, thus building the foundation for a positive mindset. The positive mindset is developed by implementing ideas that transform themselves into strong convictions.

Having a positive mindset allows us to perceive our thoughts as constructive blocks and adopt only those ideas that help us achieve our goals. This sense of achievement then grants happiness and fulfillment.

Building a positive mindset is not an inherent quality but a personal choice. You are responsible for your ownself. You have the power to train your brain and alter it to a positive attitude. Anchoring to this change shows you the path to happier, contented life.

You can build a positive mindset by following these eight techniques.

Live in the Present

The first step to building a positive mindset is to learn to focus on the present. Encourage yourself to fully cherish every shade of your amazing life. When you start living in the moment, you realize that every experience counts, however small it may feel.

You begin to enjoy something as simple as showing affection to a pet or taking a mindful walk.

We talked about the different ways to live in the moment previously. Start implementing them, and you'll find it easier to embrace the present and enjoy it.

Concentrate on the Good Things in Life

The next step is to make yourself believe that you are a positive person. If you think positively, you act positively.

Simply start behaving like a positive person, and it will slowly change your attitude towards yourself and the world you live in.

Focus on the good and positive things happening to you. Listen to positive podcasts and audiobooks, read inspirational stories, and encircle yourself with positive images and motivational objects when you are at home so that you feel content or inspired.

Every time you face a challenge, think of what it teaches you. If you are stuck in a traffic jam, use that time as an opportunity to tune into your favorite radio station, meditate, practice gratitude, and more. If a business deal didn't go well, perhaps, it is a chance for you to improve your work. When you focus on the positives, even challenging situations become easier for you.

Practice Gratitude

Gratitude refers to being thankful for your life and all the blessings in it. If you just take out five minutes of your day to intentionally adopt the habit of appreciation, it will surely affect your overall mindset. It nurtures contentment, happiness, and peace of mind, so you appreciate what you have and worry less about what you don't.

Start maintaining a gratitude journal for this purpose, and daily, list five things that you are grateful for. You can write anything that makes you happy and thankful towards life. For example, you may pen down a meaningful conversation you have with a family member or friend. It can be something charming you found in nature or an achievement you made at work. Thinking about what you're thankful for can immediately lift your mood, and to practice gratitude as a habit, you'll see long-term benefits.

Surround Yourself with Positive People

Always surround yourself with positive people. If you seek help to transform your mindset, that's fine. Look for people around you who always say some nice and positive words to you and lift you. Ask for advice from them and follow it.

Choose your friends wisely. It is imperative to make friends with people who are lively, optimistic, and compassionate. Socializing with these people invigorates your soul and grants you the capacity to appreciate, as you will get to hear and see people who are having it rough than you are, something that will, undoubtedly, make you start appreciating your life. Mostly, positive people nurture sturdy, caring relationships. Instead of staying around toxic influences, replace them with uplifting people.

Pay attention to how different people in your life affect you, and slowly distance yourself from the negative influences.

Share Positivity with Other People

Spreading happiness to others makes you feel good about yourself and gives you a chance to be kind to them. In a 2017 study by Oxford University, researchers concluded that practicing acts of kindness just for seven days had a quantifiable, positive effect on wellbeing, so start being kinder to those around you.

It doesn't take much to be nice to others if only you try. You could begin with complimenting your sister for her dress, thanking your coworkers for completing a tricky project, or even congratulating someone on an excellent presentation.

Look for people to help out, do volunteer work in the community, and lend a hand to those in need, and you will automatically feel more positive.

Practice Positive Self-talk

Technically speaking, self-talk is a 'dialogue' with yourself which involves understanding feelings and emotions, building perception, controlling evaluations and convictions, and recommending yourself instructions and reinforcements".

Simple as it is, self-talk is your inner conversation and is shaped by your subconscious mind, thoughts and emotions. Keeping it in mind, positive self-talk is speaking to yourself in a kind, compassionate and encouraging way. Optimistic people are more likely to indulge in positive self-talk. In contrast, pessimists may practice more negative self-talk.

Positive self-talk is a concept that seems insignificant but the truth is that it makes a lot of difference.

It offers a lot of benefits, some of which include:

- Improves satisfaction from your life

- Helps build immunity

- Enhances liveliness

- Reduces pain

- Relieves stress

- It makes cardiovascular health better

- Boosts physical wellbeing

Oftentimes, we speak negatively to ourselves, reminisce our mistakes, demean ourselves and make fun of our own ideas. This is why we feel so hurt and struggle to find our true self. To turn this around, start nurturing positive self-talk.

- Carefully observe the negative thoughts you have about yourself and write them down.

- Acknowledge yourself for highlighting those concerns.

- Then consciously replace that thought with something positive. 'I feel hurt all the time' can be changed to, 'I feel better with each passing day.'

- Repeat the new thought a few times to rewire your mind to think positively.

- When you face a tough situation or task, speak to yourself in a compassionate way like you would to a friend if they were in the same situation

- If you're on social media, unfollow anyone who somehow triggers your negative self-talk or makes you question your worth.

Work on these practices consistently to feel positive and confident in yourself.

Start Every Day on A Positive Note

Starting your day on a positive note can enhance your productivity. It can be any small gesture such as being thankful for any one of your blessings, saying something positive to yourself, or simply smiling.

Write down a positive message on a sticky note such as, 'Be happy', 'Smile', I love myself' or 'I am confident' and attach it to your computer screen at work. It can be an inspirational quote you like, a reminder to smile, or any other thing you have to be thankful for. Every time you work on your computer, you get a reminder to be kind to yourself, something that helps you stay optimistic.

Another important technique is to note down your positive experiences. Keep these notes in a crystal jar, box, or container. When you feel down, you'll experience a gush of positive vibes and memories to cherish.

Identify Your Weak Areas

Pay attention to any aspects of your personality that weigh you down or trigger your negativity. Perhaps, you have a habit of procrastination, and every time you delay an important task, you feel bad about yourself, which triggers negative thinking.

Identify all such areas and also brainstorm ways to overcome them. For instance, to overcome procrastination, break a big task into smaller steps and take the first step instantly.

Similarly, work on your negative areas one by one to become a refined version of yourself.

Now that you're ready to plunge on this inspirational journey of changing your attitude and mindset, keep in mind the simple rule: believe, act and make it happen against all odds!

Chapter 4: Reflect on Yourself

"There is no greater journey than the one that you must take to discover all of the mysteries that lie within you." – Michelle Sandlin

This century is the age of gadgets. At any time in the day, either you are using a smartphone, watching television, or playing games on a PlayStation. There is nothing wrong with it. However, excessive usage of technology leaves less space for you to reflect on yourself and find out who you truly are. We get carried away by the daily grind to the extent that we fail to contemplate on our genuine needs and aspirations.

Self-reflection is thinking about who you are and what you really want to do in life. It is the process of creating self-awareness by concentrating on what's going on in your life in a mindful and unbiased way. It is an attempt to relate with yourself and become aware of your connection with society and nature. Slowly, the process reveals the hidden truths and teaches you to listen to your inner voice.

Why Self-Reflection?

Knowing yourself allows you to take the reins of your life. It is a fundamental step for your personal growth. Self-reflection is a never-ending journey that helps you figure out your genuine self as well as your inner calling, so you start to live with purpose. Regular self-reflection practice can make you a better person— both personally and professionally.

Self-reflection is one of the many secrets of success. It is important because:

- It allows you to learn from your own mistakes. If you don't reflect on your mistakes, you are destined to repeat them. Reflecting on your past mistakes helps you figure out what went wrong and how you can avoid it in the future.

- It helps you make sense of things. By regularly engaging in self-reflection activities, you can deeply understand your thoughts and the behavior of others.

- It is a tool to uncover breakthroughs. You can find your hidden talents under self-exploration and self-discovery.

- It enables you to recognize change & track progress. You can monitor your performance with your personal goals.

- It challenges your thoughts and inner beliefs. When you take the time to reflect upon your perceived weaknesses and embarrassing moments, you realize what you tell yourself about yourself is not always true.

- It inspires self-acceptance and increases self-awareness. You come to know yourself more deeply hence becoming comfortable with who you are.

- It makes you live with pure intention and awakened conscience. You carefully watch what you do as per your moral principles.

- It enables you to relate more closely with others and help them. You can share your learning and experience with people going through the same things. You see how powerful and incredible you feel to inspire them.

- It makes you feel happy and fulfilled. If you reflect on the good things you did, you get a chance to know the brighter side of yourself and celebrate every little success.

- It grants you a perspective, and that's a good thing. Often, you are so busy and under pressure to complete a project that it overwhelms you. But if you take a minute to lay back and reflect on your daily work, it can calm you down and reduce your stress levels.

What Helps You in Self-Reflection?

Neil Thompson suggests a six steps formula for self-reflection in his famous book, "People Skills":

1. **Reading**– You must read around the topics that interest you and learn to reflect on what you read.

2. **Asking**– Ask questions to yourself and others about how they do things and why.

3. **Watching**– Observe keenly what is happening around you.

4. **Feeling** – Be aware of your emotions, what triggers them, and how you manage them. Pay attention to negative ones.

5. **Talking** –Express yourself meticulously and share your views and experiences with others.

6. **Thinking** - Learn to spend valuable time in thinking and brainstorming.

How to Make Self- Reflection a Daily Habit

If self-reflection isn't something that you do regularly, you have to train yourself to make it a habit. Here are some suggestions to do that:

- **Keep a one-sentence journal.**

If you've tried journaling in the past but failed at it, start with a one-sentence journal. Try to do it at the same time and same place, every day. Just take a few minutes at the end of every day to reflect on your day and write it down in one sentence. It helps you crystalize your reflections, and you will love it.

At the end of the week, go through the accounts and briefly summarize how you have felt. You are likely to find something prominent or extraordinary in those accounts, and soon you will notice certain pertains to connect the dots and find your true self.

- **Spend Valuable Time in Thinking**

Think deeply about yourself, your work, and your life. Take a look back at your day and reflect on what you did right and wrong in your work and your life, and see how it could be improved. Needless to say, write all of that down or record yourself speaking about it, so you go through it again to analyze yourself better.

- **Write about it publicly**

You can post your reflections on a blog, public forum, or on a social media account viewable to friends. By doing this, you are holding yourself accountable to a group of people. When you share your reflections with others, you'll feel a positive public pressure to keep it up as people expect to read them daily.

While doing all of the above, here are some questions you should explore:

1. *Who are you?*

It is a simple and reflective exercise. You can practice it with someone else or you can do it on your own. You have to repeatedly answer a question: "Who are you?" It is pretty easy: one person asks, "Who are You?" and the other answers whatever comes to mind immediately.

After each answer, the same question is asked. This continues for two minutes, and then roles switch. The person who answered earlier now gets a chance to ask, "Who are you?" Reflect on the exercise carefully. How do you view your identity? Do you associate it with your profession or relationship status? Did any answer surprise you? What did you discover about yourself? Did it remind you of any hidden truth or forgotten fact about who you truly are?

If you want to practice it alone, stand in front of a mirror and ask yourself, 'Who am I' and note down the answers you get.

2. *Monitor your inner voice*

Language has a profound impact on our relationship with ourselves and other people and things. Pay attention to the words that you use every day. Listen to your inner voice. Talk to yourself often and take suggestions from your inner self. Talking to yourself is a natural way to stimulate self-reflection, increasing motivation, and connecting with your emotions.

3. *Your superpower*

Most humans tend to ponder on the bad things about themselves. Accepting your whole self, including flaws, is imperative for self-appreciation. Write down your one superpower every day. Start with only one first, and then make a full list of all of your strengths and weaknesses. This exercise helps you to reconnect with your negative and positive sides. You understand that no one is either good or bad but what matters is how you use your strengths and weaknesses to help you or harm you.

4. *Write morning pages*

Writing morning pages is an effective and useful exercise to generate insights and resolve your problems. Immediately after you wake up, pick a piece of paper and write everything that comes to your mind. The purpose is to declutter your mind, so be honest with yourself and do not filter anything. Set your creativity free by letting your words flow without being rational.

Once you are done with it, pick another piece of paper and pen down your goal: what you'll do, when you'll do it, where, and how. Set a reminder in your phone with the morning alarm so that you can make this exercise a habit by doing the same thing at the same time and in the same place daily. It helps you to release your emotions and explore ideas that were at an unconscious level. You can preserve these pages as a source of inspiration for later on.

5. Perception/Reality

Think of the top five words that describe who you are in your opinion. Then ask ten people from your friends, family, and colleagues to do

the same thing and prepare their lists. It's better to send their lists via email or text instead of doing it in person – it ensures they don't feel judged. Compare their responses with the words on your list. The motive behind this exercise is to match up your self-image with others' opinions.

At least once a day, and more often several times a day, you must reflect on every aspect of your life, including your personality, work, and relations. You can continuously improve through this habit of reflection. It is highly recommended you develop the daily practice of reflection in your way if you haven't yet. It will have thoughtful changes in your life.

As you start to discover yourself better, start implementing the findings in your routine and life to improve your lifestyle. Let us talk about it next.

Chapter 5: Build A Meaningful Life for Yourself

Your time in this world is all that you have in your hands. Your life is limited to how long your body continues to function perfectly. Being aware of your mortality, you should strive to live this life to the fullest rather than unthankfully throwing it away just because it has harsh times.

Any challenge that you encounter in your life should not be viewed as a setback because only the good things that happen to you matter in the end. A successful career, a loving family, and a thriving social network combined may appear as the recipe for an ideal life. However, even if you check each of those boxes, you might feel like something is missing—and that "something" is the meaning of life.

A 2010 study published in *Applied Psychology* established that individuals with high levels of meaningful well-being have a sense of purpose along with a sense of control and a feeling like what they do is worthwhile. That's why they tend to live longer. Other researchers found that wellbeing might protect you by maintaining health. People with the most solid well-being are 30% less likely to die throughout the 8 ½ year follow-up period.

Find your Life's Purpose

"Finding your purpose" is more than just an idea or a dream that you will never fulfill. It's a tool for a better, happier, healthier life, but only a few people make use of it. A lack of meaning or purpose in your life causes boredom. It hinders you from seeing value in your personal and professional life, translating into high levels of stress, anxiety, depression, and other common mental disorders.

Now that you have started reflecting on yourself almost daily, think of what you are meant to do. Ask yourself questions such as, 'What is my inner calling?', 'What brings me pure joy?', 'What can I not compromise on or live without?', 'Where am I heading?', 'What do I see myself doing 20 years from now?' and similar questions.

Take your time with each of those, write down their answers and reflect on them deeply. Also, think of your skills, things that bring you joy, and what you feel aspired to do. Find a connection amongst all these elements about the answers you noted down earlier. It will take time, but you will discover your purpose soon if you regularly work on this aspect.

Set Right Goals for Yourself

A goal is a target toward which your efforts are directed. Once you have clarity on your purpose, set meaningful goals pertaining to it. These could be personal, professional, spiritual, health-related, etc.

Make sure to peg a deadline to a goal, so you know when it is due, and make it as specific as you want. Instead of thinking, 'I want to be a writer,' specify what kind of writer you wish to be and what niche or genre you want to venture into.

Once your goal is set, please do not leave it hanging. Attach a plan to it so you have some direction of how to go about your target. Think of the different tasks required to achieve that goal and then create a monthly and weekly schedule with fixed deliverables. Work on 2 to 3 high-priority tasks every day, so that you start to reach different milestones.

Sleep Well

Good quality sleep is crucial for your mental and physical health. It affects your immunity and substantially impacts your mood, temper, concentration, thinking, appetite, weight, and more. Luckily, there are specific ways to <u>get a better night's sleep</u>.

- Ensure your room is peaceful and has just the right amount of lighting (dim or bright), which helps you sleep easily.

- Don't watch tv or use a laptop/ phone in bed as the blue rays emitted from the screens disrupt your sleep cycle.

- Please do not eat or exercise before sleep as it makes you active, making it difficult for you to sleep.

- Sleep only in the bedroom, so you associate it with sleep and quickly initiate sleep whenever you lie down in it.

- Keep your occupational activities outside of the bedroom.

- Most importantly, set a fixed sleeping and rising time that allows you to sleep for 7 to 9 hours at night, and stick to it for two weeks even if you toss and turn throughout the night. Soon, your body will adjust to the routine, and you'll start getting enough shut-eye.

Eat Healthy

Food is an essential part of your life. To maintain good health, you have to be cautious about what you eat. Clean eating is a new health phenomenon nowadays.

Here are a few tips regarding your diet:

- Eat more vegetables, especially leafy greens, as they are packed with vitamins and antioxidants that boost your immunity.

- Increase intake of fruits to consume natural sugars and get a good dose of fiber, vitamins, and minerals.

- Cook more meals at home and avoid processed foods to keep your body clean of processed and harmful chemicals.

- Drink a lot of water. Keeping hydrated maintains energy levels and counters headaches, among other dehydration effects.

Moreover, whenever you are eating or drinking, remember to do so mindfully to enjoy what you eat and drink and to feel anchored at the moment.

Exercise Regularly

Regular exercise keeps you fit and boosts your energy. It is good for your physical and psychological state. One of the best times to reflect on yourself is during exercise. Utilize that time to think about your life and your work. Some of the best ideas come during walks or runs. Make a daily appointment with yourself and don't miss it.

Besides using exercise to reflect on yourself, understand that it boosts the production of mood-improving hormones, aka endorphins that make you feel happy, confident, and excited. Naturally, you feel better about yourself and your life in general when you are emotionally stable.

Pick any rigorous activity that you enjoy and engage in it for 10 minutes daily. It could be Pilates, a brisk walk, jog, swimming, basketball, or anything else. Slowly, increase the duration by a few minutes to start working out for 30 minutes 4 to 5 times a week.

Stick to the practice for a month, and you'll be amazed at how energetic, strong, and positive you feel.

Donate Your Time, Money, or Talent

If there's just one habit that can fill your life with meaning and purpose, it would be helping others. Researchers at Stanford and Florida State University discovered that meaningfulness and happiness overlap but are different. Happiness is linked to being a taker before a giver, whereas meaningfulness comes with being a giver more than a taker.

Being a "giver" in a relationship connects people. Whether you decide to spend two Saturdays in a foster home or volunteer to take your elderly neighbor to the hospital once a month, doing something considerate for others can make you feel like your life has a purpose. Your job may bring the ability to afford or support a cause with your money, or you may think to donate time to a cause you feel passionate about.

Do Things You Love and Enjoy

Sometimes, it is hard to recognize the things you feel passionate about. You may like many different things but have become so busy in the routine chores that you fail to make time for them. This is the reason why you don't feel connected to yourself in this chaotic world.

Bring a change to this practice by taking out time for things you enjoy. Explore your interests and find out what moves you and motivates you. Write down all the ideas and activities, and start engaging in them. Perhaps, you could do yoga on Mondays, go horse riding on Tuesdays, and meet your friends on Wednesdays. When you start doing things you love, life suddenly becomes a whole lot better!

Conclusion

We have come to the end of the book. Thank you for reading, and congratulations on reading until the end.

Finding yourself in this crazy world may seem tricky, but it actually isn't. If you stick to the guidelines in this book, you'll soon discover a newfound sense of happiness in you. You will start being more of yourself and find joy all around you.

If you found the book valuable, can you recommend it to others? One way to do that is to post a review on Amazon. Reviews help spread the word out about your experience with the book so that others can make an informed decision. They also help me grow as an author.

Please leave a review for this book on Amazon by visiting the page below:

https://amzn.to/2VMR5qr

Thank you, and good luck!

Emily

Printed in Great Britain
by Amazon